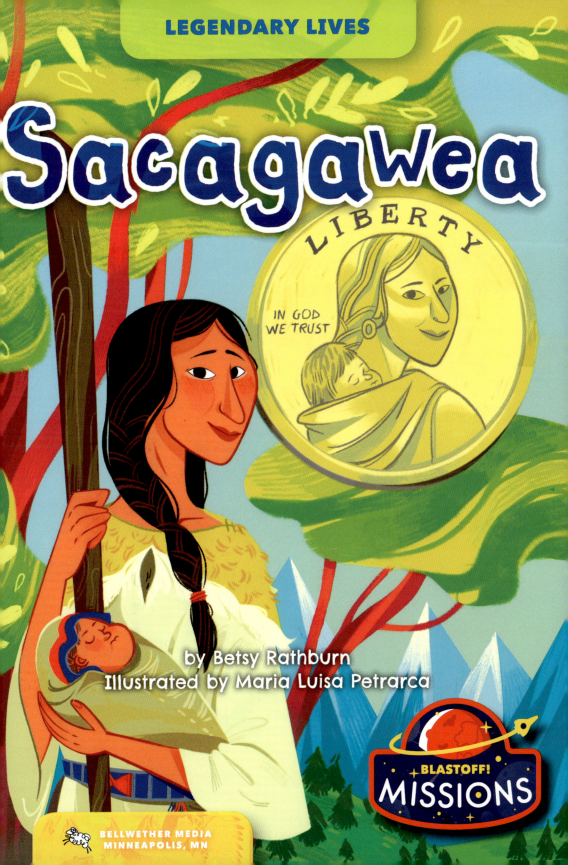

Blastoff! Missions takes you on a learning adventure! Colorful illustrations and exciting narratives highlight cool facts about our world and beyond. Read the mission goals and follow the narrative to gain knowledge, build reading skills, and have fun!

Traditional Nonfiction

Narrative Nonfiction

Blastoff! Universe

MISSION GOALS

> FIND YOUR SIGHT WORDS IN THE BOOK.

> LEARN ABOUT SACAGAWEA'S ROLE IN THE LEWIS AND CLARK EXPEDITION.

> LEARN HOW SACAGAWEA BECAME AN INSPIRATION FOR WOMEN'S RIGHT TO VOTE.

This edition first published in 2025 by Bellwether Media, Inc.

No part of this publication may be reproduced in whole or in part without written permission of the publisher. For information regarding permission, write to Bellwether Media, Inc., Attention: Permissions Department, 6012 Blue Circle Drive, Minnetonka, MN 55343.

Library of Congress Cataloging-in-Publication Data

LC record for Sacagawea available at: https://lccn.loc.gov/2024041935

Text copyright © 2025 by Bellwether Media, Inc. BLASTOFF! MISSIONS and associated logos are trademarks and/or registered trademarks of Bellwether Media, Inc.

Editor: Rebecca Sabelko   Designer: Andrea Schneider

Printed in the United States of America, North Mankato, MN.

This is **Blastoff Jimmy**! He is here to help you on your mission and share fun facts along the way!

Table of Contents

Meet Sacagawea	4
A Young Mother	6
To the Pacific	12
Journey's End	18
Glossary	22
To Learn More	23
Beyond the Mission	24
Index	24

Meet Sacagawea

Everyone in the **expedition** is hungry. Sacagawea looks for food to eat.

She collects wild vegetables. Her knowledge keeps everyone fed!

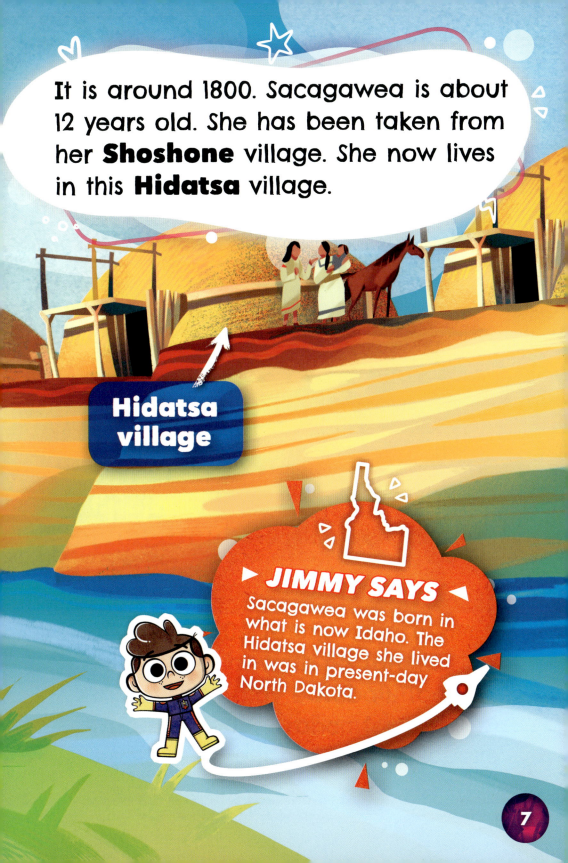

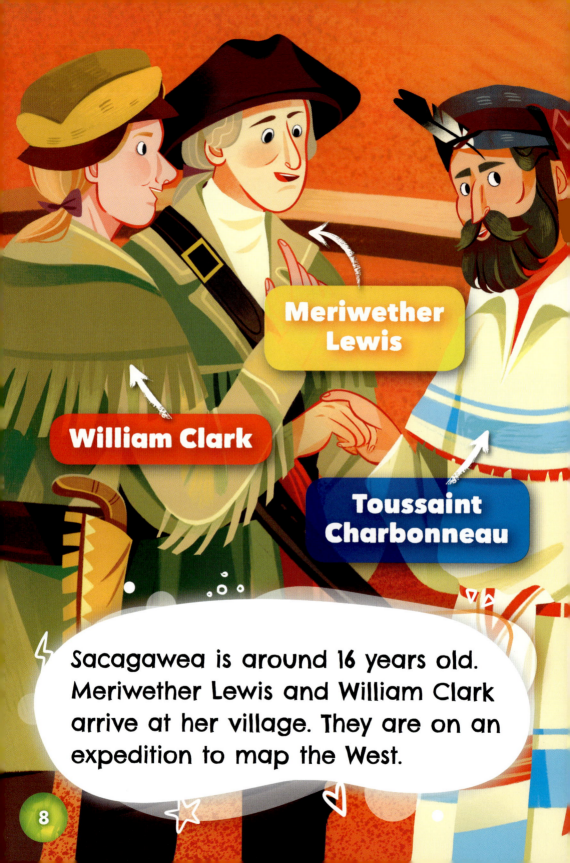

Meriwether Lewis

William Clark

Toussaint Charbonneau

Sacagawea is around 16 years old. Meriwether Lewis and William Clark arrive at her village. They are on an expedition to map the West.

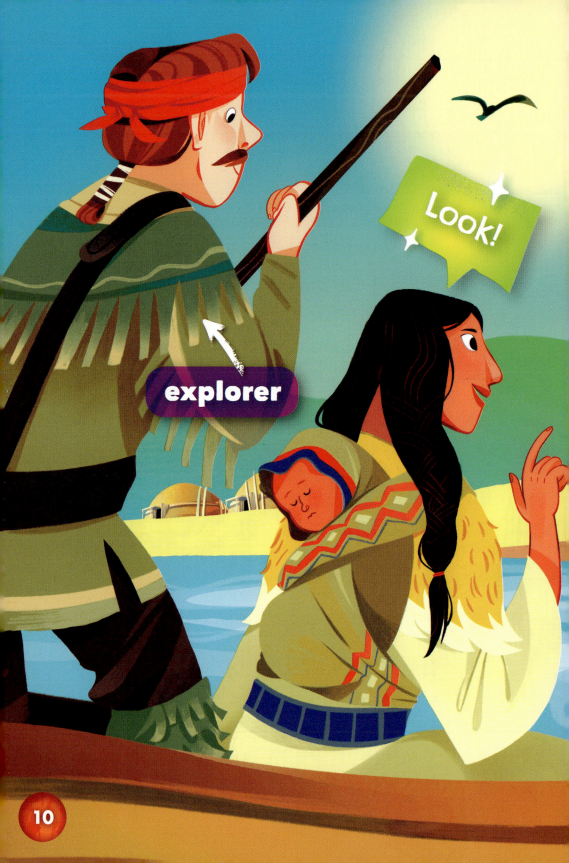

Sacagawea is now a mother. She carries her son as she travels with the **explorers**.

People they meet see her as a sign of peace. She helps keep the group safe.

To the Pacific

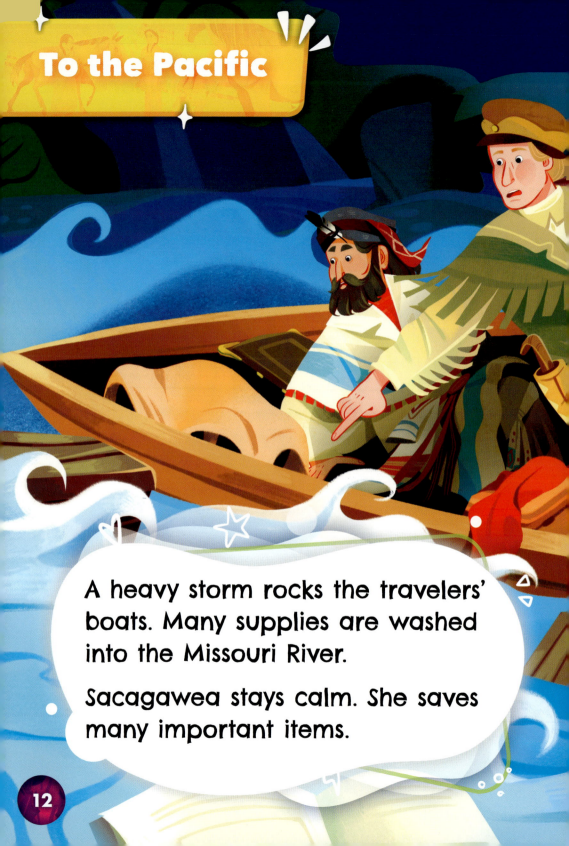

A heavy storm rocks the travelers' boats. Many supplies are washed into the Missouri River.

Sacagawea stays calm. She saves many important items.

The group has reached the Pacific Ocean. Now they must find a place to stay for the winter.

The leaders take a vote. Sacagawea helps decide.

Journey's End

The group has split up. Sacagawea guides Clark's men through the mountains.

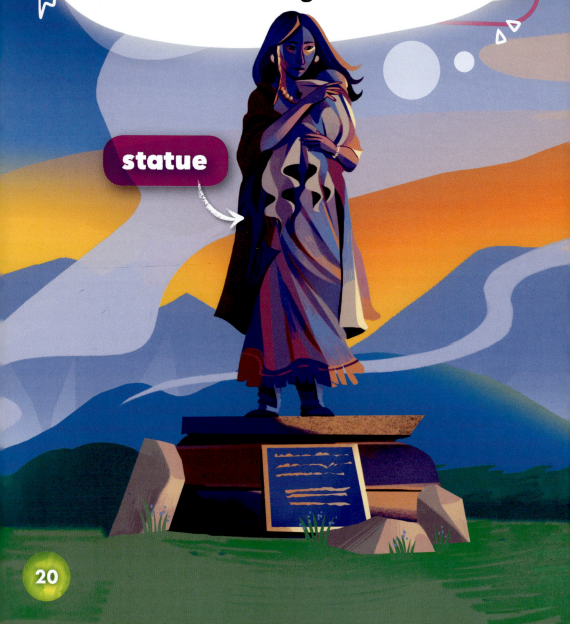

Sacagawea Profile

Born
around 1788
in present-day Idaho

Died
around December 20, 1812

Accomplishments
Shoshone woman who worked as an interpreter on the Lewis and Clark Expedition

Timeline

around 1800: Sacagawea is taken from her Shoshone village to a Hidatsa village

November 1804: Sacagawea becomes an interpreter for Meriwether Lewis and William Clark

February 1805: Sacagawea gives birth to her son, Jean Baptiste

August 1805: Sacagawea reunites with her family in Shoshone territory

November 1805: The expedition reaches the Pacific Ocean

August 1806: Sacagawea arrives back at the Hidatsa village

Glossary

demand—to strongly ask or call for something to happen

expedition—a journey by a group of people for a specific purpose, such as research

explorers—people who travel through a place in order to learn more about it or find something

Hidatsa—related to the Siouan Native American nation from the Missouri River Valley in North Dakota

inspire—to give someone an idea about what to do or create

interpreters—people who change one language into another to help people communicate

Shoshone—related to the Native American nation originally from areas of California, Idaho, Nevada, Utah, and Wyoming

territory—an area of land under the control of a certain person or group

To Learn More

AT THE LIBRARY

Chandler, Matt. *The Lewis and Clark Expedition: Separating Fact from Fiction.* North Mankato, Minn.: Capstone, 2023.

Doyle, Abby Badach. *Sacagawea.* New York, N.Y.: Enslow Publishing, 2023.

Murray, Laura K. *Sacagawea.* North Mankato, Minn.: Capstone, 2021.

ON THE WEB

FACTSURFER

Factsurfer.com gives you a safe, fun way to find more information.

1. Go to www.factsurfer.com.

2. Enter "Sacagawea" into the search box and click 🔍.

3. Select your book cover to see a list of related content.

23

BEYOND THE MISSION

› WHAT FACT FROM THE BOOK DID YOU THINK WAS THE MOST INTERESTING?

› THINK ABOUT A PERSON WHO INSPIRES YOU. WHAT DO THEY INSPIRE YOU TO ACHIEVE?

› WHAT DO YOU HOPE TO INSPIRE OTHER PEOPLE TO DO?

Index

Cameahwait, Chief, 14, 15
Charbonneau, Toussaint, 8, 9
Clark, William, 8, 18
coins, 20
expedition, 4, 8, 20
explorers, 10, 11, 19
food, 4
Hidatsa, 7
horses, 14, 15
Idaho, 7
interpreters, 9
Lewis, Meriwether, 8
Missouri River, 12
mother, 11
North Dakota, 7
Pacific Ocean, 16, 17
profile, 21
Rocky Mountains, 15, 18
Shoshone, 7, 14
statues, 20
storm, 12
supplies, 12, 13
village, 7, 8
vote, 16, 17, 20